A Day in the Life: Sea Animals

Seal

Louise Spilsbury

Heinemann Library
Chicago, Illinois

www.heinemannraintree.com
Visit our website to find out
more information about
Heinemann-Raintree books.

To order:
☎ Phone 888-454-2279
💻 Visit www.heinemannraintree.com
to browse our catalog and order online.

Edited by Sian Smith, Nancy Dickmann, and
  Rebecca Rissman
Designed by Joanna Hinton-Malivoire
Picture research by Mica Brancic
Production by Victoria Fitzgerald
Originated by Capstone Global Library Ltd
Printed and bound in China by South China Printing
  Company Ltd

14 13 12 11 10
10 9 8 7 6 5 4 3 2

**Library of Congress Cataloging-in-
Publication Data**
Spilsbury, Louise.
  Seal / Louise Spilsbury.
    p. cm.—(A day in the life: sea animals)
  Includes bibliographical references and index.
  ISBN 978-1-4329-4002-7 (hc)
  ISBN 978-1-4329-4009-6 (pb)
  1. Seals (Animals) I. Title.
  QL737.P63S65 2011
  599.79—dc22

                          2010000628

Acknowledgments

We would like to thank the following for permission to
reproduce photographs: Alamy p.12 (© Kim Westerskov);
Corbis pp.14 (© Rick Price), 22 (© Galen Rowell); FLPA
pp.15, 17, 19, 23: whiskers (Minden Pictures/Norbert
Wu), 16 (Winfried Wisniewski), 20 (Sunset), 21 (Minden
Pictures/Ingo Arndt); Getty Images pp.7, 23: flipper (The
Image Bank/Frank Krahmer), 13 (The Image Bank/Daisy
Gilardini), 18, 23: breathe (The Image Bank/Doug Allan);
Photolibrary pp.4, 23: coast (Juniors Bildarchiv), 5, 23:
Antarctica (Imagestate/Ethel Davies), 6, 23: blubber
(Animals Animals/Bradley W Stahl), 8 (Picture Press/
Thorsten Milse), 9, 23: pup (Oxford Scientific Films (OSF)/
David Tipling), 10 (Oxford Scientific Films (OSF)/Doug
Allan), 11 (Oxford Scientific Films (OSF)/Rick Price).

Cover photograph of a Seal taken in Lincolnshire, England
reproduced with permission of Corbis (Design Pics/© John
Short). Back cover photograph of a flipper reproduced
with permission of Getty Images (The Image Bank/Frank
Krahmer). Back cover photograph of whiskers reproduced
with permission of Getty Images (The Image Bank/Doug
Allan).

We would like to thank Michael Bright for his invaluable
help in the preparation of this book.

Every effort has been made to contact copyright holders
of material reproduced in this book. Any omissions will
be rectified in subsequent printings if notice is given to the
publisher.

What Is a Seal? 4
What Do Seals Look Like? 6
What Do Seals Do All Day? 8
What Do Seals Do at Night? 10
What Do Seals Eat? 12
How Do Seals Find Food? 14
What Are Seal Babies Like? 16
What Do Seals Do in Winter? 18
What Hunts Seals? 20
Seal Body Map 22
Glossary 23
Find Out More 24
Index 24

Some words are shown in bold, **like this**.
You can find them in the glossary on page 23.

elephant seals

A seal is an animal that mainly lives in the ocean.

There are many different types of seal.

Weddell seal

Seals live around **coasts** all over the world.

Weddell seals are large seals that mainly live in the icy waters of **Antarctica**.

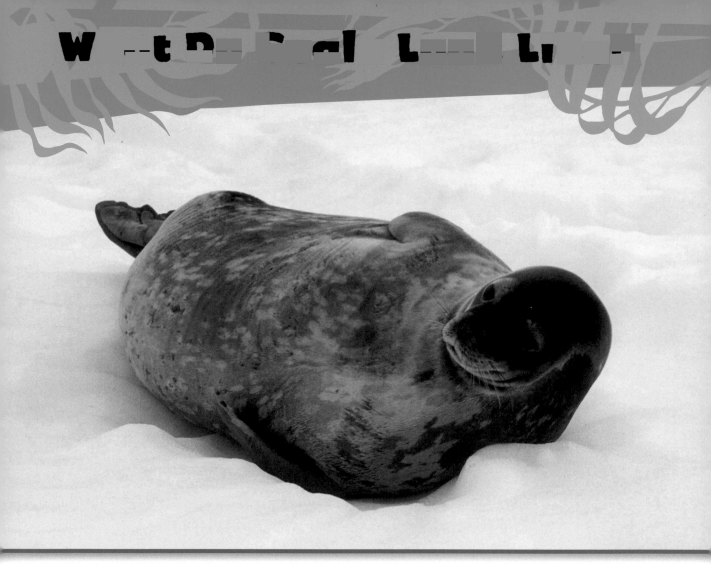

Weddell seals have black, gray, and white fur that turns brown as they get older.

They have a thick layer of **blubber** under their skin to keep them warm.

flipper

Seals' bodies are long and smooth to help them swim quickly.

They have two front **flippers** and two back flippers and a short tail.

In summer, Weddell seals spend a lot of time on the ice.

They pull themselves along on their bellies using their front **flippers**.

They rest and clean their fur with
their claws.

Weddell seals can rest in the same place
for hours.

W___t _____ ___l ____ at Night?

On summer nights, Weddell seals mainly hunt for food.

They dive through holes in the ice and swim down deep in the ocean.

It is light all day and all night in **Antarctica** in summer.

Weddell seals can see fish as the light shines through the ice.

Weddell seals catch and eat their food in the water.

They mainly eat fish and other small sea animals.

teeth

Seals have sharp teeth and claws for holding food.

They swallow fish whole or in big chunks.

Before seals dive, they close their nostrils and mouth.

They can stay underwater for about 20 minutes.

whiskers

Seals use their **whiskers** to find food in deep and dark water.

Seals can feel where fish are moving with their whiskers.

Wtr l Babies Like?

pup

Seal babies are called **pups**.

A Weddell seal pup has soft gray, brown, or golden fur.

Pups feed on milk from their mother's body.

They follow their mothers to learn how to swim, dive, and hunt.

W––t ––– ––l –– in Winter?

In winter, Weddell seals live and feed under the ice all the time.

They chew at the ice with their teeth to make holes to **breathe** through.

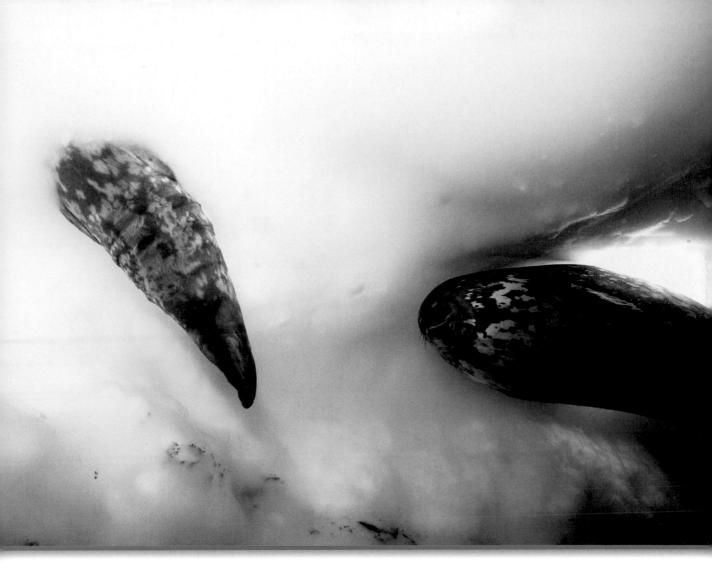

In winter, seals sleep in the water, too.

They sleep by holes in the ice so they can breathe when they need to.

In winter, Weddell seals are safe.

Life is too cold and hard in **Antarctica** for other animals that hunt Weddell seals.

leopard seal

In late summer, the ice breaks up for a while.

Killer whales and leopard seals come to hunt Weddell seals.

back flipper

whiskers

front flipper

Antarctica area around the South Pole

blubber layer of fat around a seal's body that keeps it warm in cold seas

breathe to take air into the body

coast area of land next to the sea

flipper flat part of a seal's body that it uses instead of arms for swimming

pup baby seal

whiskers long, stiff hairs that grow out of an animal's face

Fi.. --"t M--r

Books

Lindeen, Carol K. *Seals* (Pebble Plus). Mankato, Minn.: Capstone Press, 2005.

Townsend, Emily Rose. *Seals* (Polar Animals). Mankato: Minn.: Capstone Press, 2004.

Websites

Watch a video on harp seals and find out about them at: **kids. nationalgeographic.com/Animals/CreatureFeature/Harp-seals**

Listen to the noises different seals make at: **seaworld.org/animal-info/ sound-library/index.htm**

Index

Antarctica 5, 11, 20
blubber 6
breathing 14, 18, 19
feeding 12, 13, 17, 18
flippers 7, 8, 22
fur 6, 9, 16
hunting 10, 11, 12, 13, 14, 15, 17

movement 8, 10, 14, 15, 17
pups 16, 17
resting 9, 19
swimming 7, 10, 14, 17
whiskers 15, 22